streams
that lead
somewhere

streams *that lead* somewhere

poems

fareh malik

MAWEN*Z*I
HOUSE

We acknowledge the support of the Canada Council for the Arts for our publishing program. We also acknowledge support from the Government of Ontario through the Ontario Arts Council, and the support of the Government of Canada through the Canada Book Fund.

Cover art: "Ambitions" by Anette Sommerseth
Cover design by Sabrina Pignataro
Author photo by Charles Escobido
Illustrations on pp. 5, 23, and 47 by Paul Sanders

Library and Archives Canada Cataloguing in Publication

Title: Streams that lead somewhere : poems / Fareh Malik.

Names: Malik, Fareh, author.

Identifiers: Canadiana (print) 2022027150X | Canadiana (ebook) 20220271569 | ISBN 9781774150764
  (softcover) | ISBN 9781774150771 (EPUB) | ISBN 9781774150788 (PDF)

Classification: LCC PS8626.A45 S77 2022 | DDC C811/.6—dc23

Printed and bound in Canada by Coach House Printing

Mawenzi House Publishers Ltd.
39 Woburn Avenue (B)
Toronto, Ontario M5M 1K5
Canada
www.mawenzihouse.com

CONTENTS

III. ESTUARIES

the desperate feeling
of Tylenol forcing its way down
an already dry throat

this is a yarn that
unravels into the beauty of a stomach pump
but still won't let you forget
the overdose

For those waking up at the stream.

In honour of those who never got to.

Streams

Most people do not know
that your hands shake
violently as your final letter to
the world is drafted
as if the ink inside your pen knows
the words it will become
and twitches in fear—
wrists summoning
what little flight there is left
I try to describe that
the blackness my eyelids provide
in-between sweet blinks
is a fleeting high, and that
these ribs have been cold like
jail-cell bars
for as long as I can remember

then one day
I woke up barely alive
next to a trickling stream still
coughing up the river Styx onto grass
greener than I first realized

I may as well
see where this leads

I.

STREAMS

Life is like a stream, or a river. There will always be periods where it is shallow and rocky.

Chai

A white man called me that same tired word
terrorist
(don't worry, I'm used to it)
what was once an insult
has become a verbal tick in
frustration we were in line at the
7/11
and he had chai in his cup
when he leaned into spiced steam
nose first
he couldn't even recognize my scent

I Don't Cry Often, But When I Do

I
My eyes become overflowing fountain edges—
flooded from far too many wishes
that I won't get to see come true

II
it was because you said
we didn't have enough in common anymore,
and so I brewed a precipitation that
made this face a storm
staining my cheeks with puddles, desperate
that maybe in their reflection
you might see yourself in me

III
it's because the guns in my country
perform a harmony
they settle down to introduce the weeping solo
of a grieving mother
and I think about how that could have been mine

IV
it's because being with you was
like
living inside of infinity
I think it's funny that
in our death, all that is left are our skeletons
and in our farewell embrace, I left like dying,
holding you tight
reaching for the forever in your bones

V

it makes watering cans of my tear ducts;
I carved the flesh out of our memories and
buried their seeds in the corners of my mouth
hoping they grow upturned
to bloom a smile once more

VI

there is a Bruce Lee video playing, telling
me to be like water
and when I feel like I'm not brave enough
these tears are the best impersonation I can do

VII

my therapist assures me that
crying will make me feel light
and in honour of my too-proud male ancestors
I erupt into rainforest—
into century-long downpour
where my eyelashes resemble
morning dew-tinged palm leaves
and my face—new sun

VIII

the man on the corner
is yelling at me and my father
go back to your own country
but my flesh is of this,
of here
and for the next decade
I will be confused about
what home really means

Depression Is a Sleepless Bed

When the idea of home
was stripped from me
it was reduced to feelings
fleeting:
a house I could build
on the shoulder of my mother
closed eyes, a bodily meditation—
my brother's vocal vibrations
a shelter hidden
in the warmth of my father's chest
the angels on my shoulders transformed—
converted demons
who weighed me down with their whispers:
you are from nowhere
you should return to nowhere
and as I lie awake now, I think
maybe insomnia is just
making the moon your sun
maybe it's just
calling the darkness home

Sorry, Wrong Guy 1

The first time I ever had a gun pointed at
me I was on a Westbound locomotive—
at the intersection of fear and
confusion I found a crescendo,
it blasted this soul into astral
projection and through train car
windows
it saw my body at the barrel
of three police pistols

Brown Skinned and Beautiful

We are the ones who look like the soil in your
planters and the gingerbread men you make on
Christmas
the ones who are the coffee beans
your complex order from
Starbucks (we have been brewed to
a fine dust) I am someone who was
given quicksand skin—
an excuse for your harsh gaze
to sink in slow
I carry my mother's sweet, chocolate words
and my father's soot-soaked hours of labour
I am the brick for your chimneys and the
lumber sacrificed for the fire—
the spices you came to my people for
blended together in mortar and pestle
concocted the melanin that
you wished you could taste

I am the one you raised a gun at
the one you said looked like a threat
this skin was the stage where your appreciation
became fear
and from this I learned
no matter how nurturing the tree
people may still bring axes to our
trunk

After 9/11 the War Spilled into Our Hometowns & Made Us Grow Up Too Fast & My Homie's Sister Don't Wear Her Hijab No More

& all my friends on the ball team say they got my back when they overhear one of the dudes from the school across town say *I heard their team's got a fuckin' Mozlem on it* & my face stays a silent obelisk, a statued testament to normalcy as I barely hear him yo my ears have no capacity for bigotry ever since they were flooded the other day with the sounds of mosque windows smashing open to an uncensored night sky & I wanna tell this boy that *the brick they threw that day was ten times heavier than the words you're floating up into the room right now* but that remark isn't nearly enough satisfaction, so it curls up into a ball inside of me & I ball my fist into vengeful demolition—a wrecking ball winding up to do to his stomach what they did to the houses of my friends from Palestine but I don't because this ain't our part of town & I'm reminded of when my cousins got caught cutting through the wrong New York alleyway by some rednecks with a pistol & damn, I never realized that a nine millimetre barrel can look black-ocean wide when you're scared enough & yeah, sure we made it home safe but our walk back held a tragic, furious kind of silence that burned our throats like salt water whenever we tried to speak its name through a drowning rage & so we swallowed it down and plastered it to our diaphragm & for years we would taste it on our breath until one day a Lexus drives by our neighbourhood and yells out *go home you fuckin' Pakis* & we try to let it go because auntie told us to keep a low profile and uncle won't even let us wear bomber jackets because they're called *bomber jackets* and even that's too risky but there is still an angry sea in our bellies & the red light they get caught at cracks open a dam & it tempts us to run up on them & so we do & this time it's we who shatter the windows.

Perks in the Melting Pot

Well—
islamophobia ain't so bad;
when I switch out my beanie
for a kufi
I get a whole booth to myself on the train

Bright Lights

I wonder why
invisibility and depression often
walk arm-in-arm
why sadness is an unnoticed trait
and the way it brandishes such a silver tongue;
how it chameleons itself into subtlety
and makes you think that the heavy air
around you
is quite normal
it is the thing that makes
every single mirror in your home feel empty
not unlike
the way no one actually pays attention to
fireworks on their way down—
dark and fizzled
out devoid of
dazzle solemn

depression feels like
having your brightest flash, then
falling from the sky
accompanied only by your own ashes

Depression Is As Bloody a Battle As Any

I asked her about the scars on her arms
the strongest person I knew

I refused to believe it was any reason short of
that she was catching eager grenades
clasping them shut in
a prison of knuckles and fingers
shielding others—
a smile on her face, as if there was
no regard for shrapnel

or perhaps she had been washed in
the flood of catcalls
and inequality, for so long
that she finally saw windows that needed breaking
since doors refused to open;
she was the kind of person who would
smash through glass ceilings
and lick her blood clean in satisfaction

I overheard that
she stole so much opportunity from life
that death himself was furious
and as the grim reaper tried to
cut off her hands in punishment
his strikes refused to slice deep enough
his scythe broke on her Nemean lioness—
thick skin

I think she saw Trump's wall
and winced as she wrapped her
hands finger to wrist
in its unravelling
barbed-wire crown

or actually
they were probably bite marks
from wrestling crocodiles in the Nile

no—
she's the kind of person to
grab roses by the thorns
hug them tightly
and promise to love every part of them equally

she shook her head

and told me:
waged wars aren't always deafening cannons
and struggle
isn't some marvelous thing
and her battles were hushed,
overlooked
nothing but a whispered conversation
between a girl and her razors

Sloth

When the sunlight that escapes from the
blinds scorches your skin
and the floor of your bedroom becomes a swamp
murky with apathy—
your bed becomes a safe haven—
oh, such irony
to be both an
escape yet
inescapable

Sorry, Wrong Guy 2

If you didn't know
terror is an anesthetic
it sucks the life out of your limbs
as cocked handguns bark
get your hands up
fright is a pair of earplugs
that tune out police commands
and replace them with your mother's last words to
you horror is a cold day, practically freezing
it winds up a frigid right hook and
aims for your mouth
so when you st-st-stutter out that you're
innocent it barely makes it out of icy jaws
you see, if you're unlucky
fear will veil its face with "non-compliance"
and invite bullets to the masquerade

On the Last Day We Spent Together, Before You Left

I would have counted the army of indented blades of grass that once held your form. I would have carved your name into the palms of my hands and pressed your scarlet initials into tree trunks. I would have played your laugh on my iPod like my favourite album, and painted your smile into my eyelids. I would have held you like a newborn does a finger—much harder than you would expect. Al Green would be playing on the jukebox. I would have swum in my mind and tied every one of my neurons together; I would have crafted them into a safe just to keep our memories impregnable. I think I could have loved you forever. I think I could have given you a warmth that would have made the sun jealous. I would build you a spaceship. I heard that Venus rotates so slowly that I could hold your hand and we could walk forever into a sunset. I could have wrung this skin dry and made coffee from your last touch; it would have kept us awake long enough to forget that eternity doesn't always come with a guarantee. You knew that—and I know you had to leave. I just wish I could have loved you a little while longer.

Bystander

What a cowardly act
to be relentlessly by my side
unyielding
only on bright, beautiful days
but to leave as soon as the darkness
rears its familiar head

you and my shadow have a lot in common

Sorry, Wrong Guy 3

This kind of situation carries with it a
grime a bullet-hole infecting,
skin-seeping mud
which hitchhikes up your nerves and asks your
brain what you did wrong—
why you're so filthy,
and it's hardly scrubbed clean by the bitter relief
of when they say
sorry, wrong guy

II.

Rivers

Life is like a stream, or a river. There will always be periods where it is shallow and rocky, but all you have to do is keep following it downstream.

Worrisome

This one is for
the men who find
solace on the edges of
cliffs
the ones that feel peace in-between
violent folds of air
who eat lightning
and still have room for dessert
those who find themselves in pitch-black fear
and lean on their
night-vision tranquility
warriors who plunge head first
into an ocean of horizon
without double-checking the parachute

I wanna be like you one day

Aftershocks

Brown girl once taught me that
her flesh was molasses
not for its darkness, or its sweetness
but because her skin was just as thick
that's how it's gotta be to survive
brown girl only ever cooked with brown sugar
for solidarity she joked
brown girl said she still felt the anxiety of her
ancestors whenever she crossed a border
looking for checkpoints feels like
an instinct
brown girl's family hoarded;
they built castles of cardboard in the living room and
they savoured every bit of
what they could call theirs—
her family said it was because
they knew what it was like to lose a home
to have a tongue stolen
to have a culture ripped clean from their wombs

at school, white girl told us
she's one-quarter Scottish
half British
and a quarter Israeli
and asked the brown girl
"what kind of brown are
you?"

your guess is as good as mine

Cupped Hands

Five times a day
I settle into my knees
with the top of my feet kissing the
carpet I cup my hands in humility
and ask for
love and
happiness,
these angels with their
ears trained on my every
wish I hope they think I'm
enough even when I don't
sometimes I imagine
that if I was truly deemed worthy,
then they would pour blessings
in the dress of milk and
honey out of their chalices
down through the atmosphere, with
its target locked on my palms

I force the muscles in my forearms to tense
wrists at the ready
fingers tied tightly together
I'll make sure to catch
every drop

My Brother Told Me the Privileged Wouldn't Understand

My revolution was born
when I decided to arm myself to the teeth
with memories of injustice
and broken experiences
we roared stories of inequality
to ears stitched shut
we let them drink from canteens
that we filled with our tears
for them, it was too salty to bear

Coloured Boys in the Suburbs Are a Novelty

On a sweltering Tuesday, me and Dylan pack into my beat-up
minivan and bump our stereo damn near to its limits, pushing
out Lupe Fiasco and Nas records on inadvertent Caucasian ears.
The volume knob spins halfway backwards like our necks do on a
double-take when we see a cop car cuz the police here don't hide no
prejudice. We go back and forth rapping along to Illmatic; Nas told
us that the world was ours even if the white boys at school told me
to go back to my country for saying I hate the winters here. We
breakdance after school and play basketball in our off time. These are
coloured-boy territories, and here live all our homies; varying shades
of rich mocha under Ecko- and Fubu-adorned battle armour. Every
afternoon is a reminder that you gotta let your hair hang down in
your face cuz *a bandana ain't gonna do nothin' good for your image
son.* Dusk-caked asphalt drinks in the vibrations of our homebound
running footsteps as symphonies of coloured mothers fill evening
air with the trust-droughted sound of *hell no you ain't gonna sleep
over at nobody else's house tonight.* You know you're close to home
when you're greeted by the bold smell of curry and garlic filling up
the block with a confidence you haven't yet found for yourself; too
many memories of plugged noses, cocktails of laughter and disgust as
I opened my lunchbox. Listen, I know all too well that people here in
this suburb see my skin before they see I'm human; I remember that
every time I gotta shave my beard before I cross the border or pops
warns me about wearing a kufi to school because *yes son it's cool
that Muhammad Ali wears one but you're not Muhammad Ali and
we gotta be extra careful 'round these parts.* I think about the men
who snatched the hijab off of my friend's head, how they built up
temples to conformity on the land they broke her down on, how god
once gathered enough stardust to fill her form and how she is now

collapsing into herself like a dying sun. Her coloured-boy clan would gather around a lit backwoods like a campfire, telling stories of places where melanin wasn't as potent a currency as here. The coloured-boy territories don't have no border, they lie just beneath the ground of our neighbourhoods like a trench so you gotta stand twice as tall just to see your peers eye-to-eye. Suburban white folks like to say that they don't see colour as their gaze meets the brown pine-box home of a dead coloured boy while my momma still sees coloured ghosts and you ask her why she can't smile for you. She puts her head on my shoulder and her tears run down my arm like a narrow stream and I'm grateful I can tell her that I'm still here.

I'm still here.

Crescent Moon

Clothes stick to my skin
soaked through from some
concoction of anxious sweat and
tears;
have you counted how many
conscious-drenched nights it takes
to stop recognizing the rise of the
sun? I have—
the craterous moon is
a hard face to fall in love with
still, I love it all the same
it spoke to my emptiness in twilight
and told it
you don't always have to be
full to be extraordinary
trust me on this

Wrath

It always baffled me
how you could have such fire in your voice
yet
no warmth in your words

For the Other Halves That Didn't Quite Fit

I don't think loving me has ever ended
beautifully I have been an inescapable storm
and they were tents;
shelter, but—
temporary

the octave of their voices were indeed keys
that tamed downpours into trickling water

the flashes of brightness that beamed from their smiles
would put lightning to shame

they enticed thunderous explosions
to shrink into chirping birds

but eventually
the gale and tempests always came back

they told me love was about finding someone
that would have sunlight dancing at their
touch now I realize
it's actually someone
to sit with in the rain

Gluttony

You were a wide mouth
with a black hole for a stomach
whose favourite foods were
hourglasses and valentine cards

Young Poet Listens to the Switchblade Salesman

Let me tell you somethin', mans that say you don't need that/
ain't never been jumped in the back/ alley of a club, crack/
smoke claws sunken into nostrils, fat/
beats loud/ enough to drown/ out these/
fists thumping on skin is a tongue/ that speaks/
in unholy drum beats/
son, these/ people never had to hand over their J's/
and walk home, ankles painted/
every single shade of naked/
you ever seen the grim reaper and have to get your breath back on
    automatic?/
you ever had the wind hurricane out of your lungs, and then you
    gotta catch it?/

Trust me more than your cousins/
trust me more than your daddy
trust me more than your brothers/
they gon' lead you to the gutter/
you can get/ eaten alive by these blocks/
bet/ they'll stomp/ you into con/ crete/
and into tombstones—if you let 'em, these/
young kids nowadays/ rise, already headstone grey/
and clay/ skin metamorphoses; bones, and blood/
trust me young/ gun/
I've seen a thousand momma's eyes/ flood/
watering the soil
ground too salty for anything to actually bud/
look at my skin/
I am the friend who forged their thin/ arms/

into ar/chives, inking memory into tissue/
shit, you/
can even see the barber carrying his straight razor
on his walk back to the bus stop

My nephews gotta be 'bout your age/
and they got roughed up/ the other day/
it don't go away/ all this tough stuff/
when you look like us/
see, my sister got lucky
her genetics are part chameleon
they must be/ the way
her kids came home alive
but a different colour than they left/
I know Omar didn't have that
and he got killed
and his mom couldn't even say nothing at the fun/eral
her mouth just bloomed/ into flowers
like a silent offering
to a too/ late shrine/
like a thorned goodbye/
like her life was cut at the root
her jaw dropped like thirsty petals/
and it settled/ like
it knew her smile was gonna wither soon.

(When the Truth Is Bitter) Repression Is an Art

I've always had a sweet
tooth candied lies have
unfailingly gone down easier than the truth
my self-deception
has spun me tales of delectability
fooling me into thinking
that every one of my marinated breaths
should taste sweet as they
fall from my lips

Pride

Your frustration
often battled my stubbornness
a burning room
which we both refused to leave

Lost Leaves

I could never understand the
trees and how they could be so
resilient as the winter comes—
knowing they will lose a piece of themselves
yet standing tall
with the faith that it will return
and you see
there has been a mighty oak
rooted around my heart, playing pericardium
hardship as its default setting
every challenge a blizzard
every tribulation a drought
this mind has provided my
soul a state of perpetual
autumn
a cold orchard
with prayers to god echoing through its branches
hoping only that one day
I may bear fruit

An Introvert's Recovery

Some nights I enter my bedroom
and instead, find myself inside of a
store I am the sole shopper
and the sign on the counter says they sell just one thing:
peace
they accept a currency called isolation
and I've got a pocket full of bills

When We Push People Away

To those affected by
my once venomous speech:
please forgive me,
I know that at my lowest
points these syntax secretions
eroded my teeth into
whetstone
fine and jagged—
they sharpened my tongue
with every cry for help

Rashida

for my grandmother

I held hands with people
I hadn't seen in years
we treated your gravestone like a campfire
and it glowed ablaze with life
together, we sat around it;
our throats belted choruses of your heyday
we stayed warm from your memory

I hope you can see that in our
sadness you brought us happiness

I hope you witness how
sometimes a departure
can bring unity

Clouds

Every girl I have ever held hands with has said that my hands felt
like clouds. My inner pessimist tells me that they're too thick; too
clumsy. The optimist in me convinces me otherwise. He says they
meant that god blessed these palms with the feeling of heaven—that
my fingers are gates. That they could hear scripture at their touch,
and music with my grasp. That the lines in these hands are actually
paradise riverbeds, flowing endlessly with a torrent of cocoa butter.
That everyone I have ever felt has tried to read their future in my
sky. I could believe that every woman I have loved with no return
was an arid desert from the wrist down—craving nothing but rain
shower; my digits lightning bolts trying endlessly to spark interest.
These knuckles could be mountain tops for you, peaking through
thunderstorm-fists should you ever need protection. Did you know
that if we laid on hilltops and watched sapphire canvases I could
make these hands transform into anything you could imagine? I
don't know much, but I know clouds aren't all that impressive or rare.
I know, at first glance, neither am I. I know the harsh reality is this:
clouds drift, and that I've never let my joints settle in one place too
long before. But more than anything, I know that I'd like to try with
you.

Muse

They don't sell bottles of your essence at the corner store
so I can't get so drunk on you
that I produce miracles
instead, I touch your body
I let my hands soak in the oceans of
inspiration that reside beneath your skin
until my fingertips become wrinkled with creativity
I let the water drip down my pen
mix with the ink
and translate brilliance into English

Overprotective

I am slowly learning to ease my
grip on everything I fear losing
because
my overly tight grasp
has broken too many things before

III.

ESTUARIES

Life is like a stream, or a river. There will always be periods where it is shallow and rocky, but all you have to do is keep following it downstream and you'll find oceans.

Greed

Your opinion floated on air currents
whenever I inhaled
and relief sailed out of my
mouth as I exhaled
if you've ever had an asthma
attack or a panic attack for that
matter
you'd know how much you miss breathing;
how much you miss air
you would know how much I craved the oxygen
that carried your approval

no more

Wherever They Erect Statues of the Tyrants, We Will Say

Look around; they built altars out of villains. They pasted their memories into church pews and worshipped on their knees. They must have held seances in residential schools and drew prayer circles to summon the spirits of the corrupted. Slave masters. Ghosts of the oppressors. These statues were hard work. They didn't take a snapshot. It wasn't quick. It took time; they didn't just freeze evil in a brief moment of stone. They didn't make their mistakes quietly, either. I heard they screamed across battlefields as they threw blood to stone; the Earth steeped in our lives like a premature burial—'til it matched my skin and sang mama's story. I heard they stole clean water pipes and melted them down to make bayonets. They fought for these. They toiled. They worked hard. They sweated, they bled, they broke. Oh, the things they broke. They broke down our mountains. They broke our countries the way they broke stone; left in shards of its former self. They broke families. They carried boulders from the hilltops as they summoned Atlas in their bones and they prayed those didn't break too.

Heartsong

Boy,
you'd have to squint to see those
eyes bright and
vivid like a sunset
lips that taste like sunlight
and the aroma of her
embrace like a Sunday
afternoon

Flower Power

On our second date
our waitress saw my floral bandana and asked
why I loved flowers so much *they're pretty* I
said
what I should have said was:
Miss, you should have been at our first date
when I brought her a bouquet of daisies
you should have seen Isaac Newton's jaw
drop as gravity itself surrendered from her
brow and the corners of her mouth—
how her face levitated into joy
as if defying the laws of physics

I want to tell her that
I think the flowers' will to live withered a long time
ago but they set their alarm clocks
stretch out their leaves
and wake from their slumber every spring because
they know they'd get to see her face
and that's enough
I apologize to every root I pull from home
and they shake off their dirt
with nods of understanding
because it's for her

I want to tell her that
when she walks in the
park and the roses see her
every other petal that has
she loves me not
etched on its underbelly
is drained of its crimson and
turns into a white flag
that submits with apology

I wish I had told that waitress how beautiful flowers can be
when you're in love

A Temporary Faith (Unfinished)

There are half-filled, dust-tinted journals on the bookshelf that spawned in my loneliness. The number of my friends would sway like the tides; often leaving for months at a time. The same wavelengths that explained to my mom why I prayed five times a day in her sickness, then stopped altogether afterwards. It is the Icarus in me that desires melted wax wings when I have good things going. It is the reason I have loved too shallow and too short; too deeply and too long. My conviction has proved to be more short-matchstick than candle, and it still burns my hand all too often. Comfort has writhed itself around my limbs and squeezed my muscles into submission far too many times. Someone once told me that it's most important to persevere when you get comfortable. Harsh rapids are easy; I am still trying to figure out how to keep my boat moving in still waters.

Writer's Block

I hold my pen
like I hold
grudges angry,
unforgiving,
and for far too long

Amazon

for my mother

When I would hear the word *warrior*
I thought of my action figures
most often men
who had broad frames and rippling muscles
hands tethered to sword and shield

still, I never realized
that my mother was
Athena the strongest
warrior of all
she wore her pride as she did her battle scars
like badges of honour sewn into her arms
covered by sleeves which proudly housed her heart
she brewed tonics of independence
and orange
pekoe every
morning
arm-wrestling this life and its adversity at every crossroad

it wasn't until I myself walked the path less travelled
that I saw her silhouette
many miles ahead of me;
what I perceived as
hobbling—results of fatigue
from her war and the
wounds on her chest—was
actually dancing
a woman celebrating her triumphs
and the parts of her still unscathed

Duality of Me

I don't know why
but I've always loved
asymmetry things with two
halves
that weren't quite the same
as if announcing to the world that
yes I can be both of these at the
same time
and I don't care what you think

The Carpenter

I came to you
with lumber and drywall under my arms
we walked hand in hand
to where the manor of your self-esteem
once stood
ruins
demolished in its youth
by a person, unqualified and without
license I made sure you laid the foundation
yourself decorated the windows with
sunflowers
and painted the walls vibrant ochre and
caramel we built it sturdy
so it may never be torn down again

January 26, 1994

About twenty-eight years ago
when the Earth heard I was
coming it rumbled with
excitement,
while tectonic plates shifted into a
smile it toasted my arrival
holding glasses filled with
ocean water
confetti and streamers danced in the
heavens in the guise of rain and lightning
the entire planet spun around with glee

yes—I know the world spins around every 24 hours
but I know in my heart
that one was for me

Tongue of the Diaspora

My father whips his
tongue through the air
like a sword
and carves the room free from English

he tells me
my blade's gone dull

Somewhere

Most of the time

somewhere

isn't a place,
but rather
it is

here

where you
sit on a diving board of
what you used to be
trusting that the water below
outruns the ceramic tiles
to catch you

where your smile no longer
feels like aching cheeks

sometimes

somewhere

isn't a home
but it is just
existing

in rebellion of a world
that wants you to not

sometimes

somewhere

is putting that first quarter
in a piggy bank

    like your heart has finally
    changed its locks
    to something that you
    actually have the key to

        that a shower
        is no longer a temple—
        worshipping the art of
        breaking down

            when the
            grocery store's ethnic food aisle
            stops feeling like the only piece of home left

    all of this—
    somewhere

and somewhere
is where we are born

    the stones in our backpacks
    ripening–
    deciding to be mangoes instead
    blood-crusted beard, now
    chin drenched in juice

        us—still looking for oceans
        now sure
        that they're out there

somewhere.

Acknowledgements

I want to thank Mawenzi House for trusting me and seeing the potential in me and my manuscript. To Nurjehan and MG—you have been pivotal not just in the creation of this book, but in the early stages of my writing career. I also want to thank all of the journals, magazines, and platforms who gave my poems a home, and gave an emerging author a voice. I promise to use it well.

This book comes from a place of perseverance and betterment. It was born out of hope. I would not be where I am without the infinite love and support I have received from the people around me. I wouldn't be who I am without my friends and family.

Chantal, thank you for your endless supply of support—both kind and, at times, brutally honest.

To my father—thank you for your boundless innovation and guidance.

Jasim, thank you for your light. It has illuminated my darkest days.

And finally thank you to my mother, who wonderfully embodies all of the above.

Follow the stream.

Publishing Acknowledgements

"Chai," *Parentheses Journal* & *Twyckenham Notes*; "Sorry, Wrong Guy 1, 2 & 3," *86 Logic*; "Brown Skinned and Beautiful," *Parentheses Journal* & *Twyckenham Notes*; "After 9/11 the War Spilled Into Our Hometowns & Made Us Grow up Too Fast & My Homie's Sister Don't Wear Her Hijab No More," *Lucky Jefferson*; "Bright Lights," *Royal Rose Magazine*; "Depression Is As Bloody a Battle As Any," *Parentheses Journal*; "On the Last Day We Spent Together, Before You Left," *The Aurora Journal*; "Bystander," *Parentheses Journal*; "Worrisome," *Brave Voices Magazine*; "Aftershocks," *Weasel Press* & Finalist in *So To Speak*'s 2020 Poetry Contest; "Cupped Hands," placed first in Muslim Hands Canada's 2020 Poetry Contest; "My Brother Told Me the Privileged Wouldn't Understand," *Parentheses Journal*; "Coloured Boys in the Suburbs are a Novelty," *Waccamaw Journal*; "Crescent Moon," *Open Minds Quarterly*; "(When the Truth Is Bitter), Repression Is an Art," *Parentheses Journal*; "Rashida," *Ghost Heart Literary Journal*; "Clouds," *The National Arts Centre*; "Muse," *Royal Rose Magazine*; "My Great-Grandkids Will Find the Battered Remains of a Confederate Statue and Say," *Ghost Heart Literary Journal*; "Flower Power," *Parentheses Journal*; "A Temporary Faith," *Words & Whispers*; "The Carpenter," featured poem at San Antonio's McNay Art Museum; "January 26th, 1994," *Chitro Magazine*.